SPOTLIGHT ON SOCIAL AND EMOTIONAL LEARNING

THE TIES THAT BIND US TOGETHER

RELATIONSHIP BUILDING

I0883159

CHRISTINE HONDERS

PowerKiDS press.

NEW YORK

Published in 2020 by The Rosen Publishing Group, Inc.
29 East 21st Street, New York, NY 10010

Copyright © 2020 by The Rosen Publishing Group, Inc.

All rights reserved. No part of this book may be reproduced in any form without permission in writing from the publisher, except by a reviewer.

Editor: Rachel Gintner
Designer: Michael Flynn

Photo Credits: Cover Mike Harrington/Taxi/Getty Images; cover, pp. 1, 3–4, 6–8, 10–12, 14, 16, 18–20, 22–24 (background) TairA/Shutterstock.com; pp. 5–6, 19 Monkey Business Images/Shutterstock.com; p. 7 Bill Clark/CQ-Roll Call Group/Getty Images; p. 9 Iakov Filimonov/Shutterstock.com; p. 10 Pressmaster/Shutterstock.com; p. 11 Sergey Novikov/Shutterstock.com; p. 12 https://en.wikipedia.org/wiki/File:Twain1909.jpg; p. 13 https://en.wikipedia.org/wiki/Helen_Keller#/media/File:Helen_KellerA.jpg; pp. 14–15 EMkaphotos/Shutterstock.com; p. 17 Oleg Golovnev/Shutterstock.com; p. 21 Everett-Art/Shutterstock.com; p. 21 https://en.wikipedia.org/wiki/Thomas_Jefferson#/media/File:Official_Presidential_portrait_of_Thomas_Jefferson_(by_Rembrandt_Peale,_1800)(cropped).jpg; p. 22 wavebreakmedia/Shutterstock.com.

Cataloging-in-Publication Data

Names: Honders, Christine.
Title: The ties that bind us together: relationship building / Christine Honders.
Description: New York : PowerKids Press, 2020. | Series: Spotlight on social and emotional learning | Includes glossary and index.
Identifiers: ISBN 9781725306943 (pbk.) | ISBN 9781725306974 (library bound) | ISBN 9781725306950 (6pack)
Subjects: LCSH: Interpersonal communication in adolescence--Juvenile literature. | Interpersonal relations in adolescence--Juvenile literature. | Friendship in adolescence--Juvenile literature.
Classification: LCC BF724.3.I55 H66 2020 | DDC155.5'19 --dc23

Manufactured in the United States of America

CPSIA Compliance Information: Batch #CWPK20. For further information contact Rosen Publishing, New York, New York at 1-800-237-9932.

CONTENTS

CHAPTER ONE

YOUR RELATIONSHIPS

Think about the people in your class. Who are your friends? Which people do you not get along with? Your friends are probably the people with whom you have common interests. For example, you likely joke and laugh about the same things. However, everyone encounters people they don't like or agree with.

A **relationship** is a connection between two people. You probably have close relationships with people you love, such as your family and friends. You also have relationships with people you see often, such as your teacher, your neighbor, or maybe even your mail carrier.

Forming good relationships with people helps us build strong, long-lasting friendships, and having good friends often makes us feel happy and secure. Building a good relationship also means knowing that even if you don't get along all the time, you can still figure out how to work together.

It takes everyone's effort to make relationships strong. Working together is the best way forward.

CHAPTER TWO

BORN TO CONNECT

From the moment babies are born, they want to connect with someone. They figure out who's around them very early in their lives. They recognize the face and smell of their caregiver. When they hear a warm, loving voice, they know it's someone who will take care of them.

When a caregiver picks a baby up and holds them gently, the baby's learning that this person loves them. A baby depends on their caregiver to treat them well. A bond and a sense of trust often form between them.

The more time a parent and baby spend together, the greater their bond becomes. In this photo, Senator Tammy Duckworth arrives with her newborn to cast a Senate vote on April 19, 2018.

Babies also show love back to their caregivers. They smile when they hear a familiar voice. They may raise their arms to be picked up when they see them. Babies watch adults to learn how to treat others. When the adults around them are happy, helpful, and caring, babies often become that way too.

CHAPTER THREE

THE BUILDING BLOCKS

As children, we usually learn to trust the people we love. If we're lucky, we carry that feeling throughout our lives. Trust is one of the main building blocks in a relationship. Trust means feeling **confident** in the other person. You understand that they'll always have your back and won't misdirect you. You feel safe with them.

On the other hand, it can be hard to trust someone new, so it's important to think about how you **interact** with new people. Are you both being honest? Are you there for each other?

Another important building block is respect. Having respect means you think good things about a person and their **abilities**. Showing respect means letting other people know that you care about them and their feelings. It means treating people well and knowing that others have the right to look, think, or act differently than you.

Even if you don't like your parents' rules, you follow the rules because you want to show your parents that you respect them.

CHAPTER FOUR

COMMUNICATION

You can't have a relationship without good communication. Communication means sharing **information** or feelings. Good communication isn't just talking to people. It also means listening and replying to other people thoughtfully. It means encouraging them to **express** themselves. Good communication helps us start and keep relationships.

Compliments create a positive energy around people. They're especially appreciated when they're genuine, or real – such as when you compliment someone for something thoughtful they did.

It's hard to begin a **conversation** with someone you don't know. Introducing yourself with a smile is a good way to start. You could invite a new person to join your friends in a game. You could ask them what they did over the weekend. Or, you might share something about yourself, such as, "I went to basketball practice yesterday. Do you play basketball?" You may find out you like the same things.

Giving a **compliment** is also a good way to start. Complimenting someone on something they did well shows that you value them.

CHAPTER FIVE

GIVE-AND-TAKE

When you're friends with someone, you want to give the other person things they need, such as love and support. But if the other person isn't giving back, it doesn't feel good.

Good relationships are based on give-and-take. In a friendship, you want to give the other person what they need because you care about them. If the other person respects and cares for you, they'll do the same thing. But if one of you takes more than you give, the relationship will have problems.

For instance, if you see that a friend is sad, you might go and talk to them to make them feel better. You give them attention and a friendly ear. If the next time you're sad, they avoid you and don't try to comfort you, they're not doing their part.

MARK TWAIN

Helen Keller and author Mark Twain were great friends. Keller said of Twain that he treated her like a real person and always listened to her.

HELEN KELLER

CHAPTER SIX

BEING CONSIDERATE

Being considerate is being polite and caring toward others. It means you're careful to avoid hurting people or purposefully making them feel bad. Good manners, such as saying please and thank you, are part of being considerate. It also means taking turns during games. It means you share with others. You speak to other people without interrupting or taking over. Being considerate of others' feelings is a big part of good relationships.

Being considerate of other people's opinions is also very important. It's impossible for people, even best friends, to agree on everything. When you're in a disagreement with a friend, there are ways to communicate without attacking them and making them feel bad. Instead of saying, "You're wrong!" you might say, "I understand what you're saying but this is what I think." You can even agree to disagree!

If your relationship is built on trust and communication and you're considerate and respectful to each other, you can work out almost any problem.

CHAPTER SEVEN

PATIENCE

In a relationship, each person must have patience. You have to learn to take turns and let the other person go first sometimes when you're playing together. Being patient means being able to wait for what you want.

Patience is also important when you're communicating. It's no fun talking to someone who doesn't stop talking about themselves. It makes you feel less important. Letting the other person have a chance to reply shows you care about how they feel.

Part of being patient means having self-control. This means thinking about what you're going to do or say before acting on **impulse**. Some kids act out when they're angry. They hit people or call them names. They don't think before they react. It's better to stop and think, take a deep breath, and calmly explain why you're upset.

If you find yourself losing your patience and getting angry, a good way to cool off is to walk away from the annoying situation. You won't lose your temper, and it might make you feel better.

CHAPTER EIGHT

PUTTING YOURSELF IN THEIR SHOES

Part of building a relationship means having perspective, or the ability to see things from another person's point of view. That means putting yourself in someone else's shoes and understanding how they feel and why. You might think about how you would act in that situation.

Understanding other people's perspectives is one key to a good relationship. Can you see why your friend might be sad or why they might be happy? With perspective, you might be able to **predict** what they'll do or say based on their point of view. You might notice how their behavior affects other people around you.

People with perspective know that it's important to consider other people's feelings. They may change their behavior so they don't **offend** others. They think very carefully about how to say something before they say it.

It's even more important to have perspective when we have relationships with people from families and backgrounds different than ours. Differences are an opportunity to learn something new or gain a new perspective.

CHAPTER NINE

WHEN RELATIONSHIPS GO WRONG

No one gets along all the time. We sometimes fight with even our best friends. But if we use the right tools, we can get through conflicts with our friends without losing those friends.

When there's a problem, communicate! Tell your friend how you feel and let your friend express themselves without interrupting them. Pay attention and listen–maybe you did something that bothered them, and you didn't even realize it. Don't use hurtful words. And if you did something wrong, **apologize**. If you have trust, you can forgive, forget, and still be friends.

For example, if one of your friends doesn't want to play that day, think of a positive way to turn it around. You might think, "If Abby doesn't want to play tag with me today, I'll find someone else to play with. Greg loves tag. And maybe Abby will want to play tag tomorrow."

Founding Fathers John Adams and Thomas Jefferson often disagreed about politics. However, they repaired their friendship as they grew older by writing to each other.

JOHN ADAMS

THOMAS JEFFERSON

CHAPTER TEN

GOOD RELATIONSHIPS LAST A LIFETIME!

You'll be meeting new people for the rest of your life. Having the skills to build relationships may help you make friends, but you'll also be able to work more effectively with your classmates in school, your teammates in a sport, or other workers at your job. You'll know how to communicate and listen. You'll pay attention to how other people are feeling. You'll be able to share ideas and get along.

Knowing how to build and keep good relationships will make you feel better about yourself. Other people will think well of you, too! They'll know you're someone they can trust and someone who will respect their feelings.

There's no way you can be friends with everyone you meet, but at least you'll know how to get along with them. And if you build good relationships with friends and family, they'll stick with you for a long, long time.

GLOSSARY

ability (uh-BIH-luh-tee) The power or skill to do something.

apologize (uh-PAH-luh-jiyz) To say you're sorry for something said or done.

compliment (KAHM-pluh-muhnt) A remark that says something good about someone or something, or to make such a remark.

confident (KAHN-fuh-duhnt) Having a feeling of trust or belief that you can do something well.

conversation (kahn-vuhr-SAY-shuhn) Talking with other people; using your words to communicate with others.

express (ik-SPRES) To make one's thoughts and feelings known.

impulse (IHM-puhls) A sudden desire to do something.

information (in-fuhr-MAY-shun) Knowledge or facts about something.

interact (ihn-tuhr-AKT) To come together and have an effect on one another.

offend (uh-FEND) To cause to be angry or annoyed.

predict (prih-DIKT) To guess what will happen in the future based on facts or knowledge.

relationship (rih-LAY-shun-ship) The way in which two or more people are connected.

INDEX

PRIMARY SOURCE LIST

Page 7
U.S. Senator Tammy Duckworth and newborn in Washington, D.C. Photograph. April 19, 2018. Bill Clark.

Page 12
Mark Twain. Photograph. 1907. A. F. Bradley.

Page 13
Helen Keller. Photograph. ca. 1904.

Page 21
John Adams. Painting. ca. 1800 to 1815. Gilbert Stuart.

Page 21
Thomas Jefferson. Painting. 1800. Rembrandt Peale.

WEBSITES

Due to the changing nature of Internet links, PowerKids Press has developed an online list of websites related to the subject of this book. This site is updated regularly. Please use this link to access the list: www.powerkidslinks.com/SSEL/relationship